Dad

• IN A •
MILLION

summersdale

DAD IN A MILLION

An Hachette UK Company
www.hachette.co.uk

Summersdale Publishers Ltd
Part of Octopus Publishing Group Limited
Carmelite House
50 Victoria Embankment
LONDON
EC4Y 0DZ

www.summersdale.com

Printed and bound in Malta

ISBN: 978-1-78685-763-7

Substantial discounts on bulk quantities of Summersdale books are available to corporations, professional associations and other organizations. For details contact general enquiries: telephone: +44 (0) 1243 771107 or email: enquiries@summersdale.com.

TO............................

FROM............................

LIFE DOESN'T COME WITH AN INSTRUCTION BOOK; THAT'S WHY WE HAVE FATHERS.

H. JACKSON BROWN JR

"

My father gave me the greatest gift anyone could give another person: he believed in me.

JIM VALVANO

"

A father is a giant
from whose shoulders
you can see forever.

PERRY GARFINKEL

DAD TAUGHT ME EVERYTHING I KNOW. UNFORTUNATELY, HE DIDN'T TEACH ME EVERYTHING HE KNOWS.

AL UNSER JR

A TRULY RICH MAN IS ONE WHOSE CHILDREN RUN INTO HIS ARMS WHEN HIS HANDS ARE EMPTY.

NOBLE
FATHERS
HAVE NOBLE
CHILDREN.

EURIPIDES

MY DAD IS
MY HERO. I'M
NEVER FREE OF A
PROBLEM, NOR DO I
TRULY EXPERIENCE
A JOY UNTIL WE
SHARE IT.

NANCY SINATRA

My father didn't tell me
how to live; he lived, and
let me watch him do it.

CLARENCE BUDINGTON KELLAND

A FATHER IS A MAN WHO EXPECTS HIS SON TO BE AS GOOD A MAN AS HE MEANT TO BE.

FRANK A. CLARK

Other things may change us, but we start and end with family.

ANTHONY BRANDT

THINGS DADS CAN DO WITH ONE HAND BEHIND THEIR BACK

Carry the family's luggage
(including three suitcases
and a deckchair)

Always find a spot to park the car

Carry sleeping children up to
bed without waking them

Build the coolest den from
a load of old junk

Simultaneously drink beer,
eat snacks and keep other
people's hands away
from the TV remote

WHEN I WAS A KID, I USED TO IMAGINE ANIMALS RUNNING UNDER MY BED. I TOLD MY DAD... HE CUT THE LEGS OFF THE BED.

LOU BROCK

Dads are stone skimmers, mud wallowers, water wallopers, ceiling swoopers, shoulder gallopers, upsy-downsy, over-and-through, round-and-about whooshers.

HELEN THOMSON

DAD: A SON'S FIRST HERO, A DAUGHTER'S FIRST LOVE.

ANONYMOUS

HAVING ONE CHILD MAKES YOU A PARENT; HAVING TWO YOU ARE A REFEREE.

DAVID FROST

Ask your mother.

I APPRECIATE
EVERYTHING
YOU DO

for me.

MY DADDY, HE WAS SOMEWHERE BETWEEN GOD AND JOHN WAYNE.

HANK WILLIAMS JR

The raising of a child is the building of a cathedral. You can't cut corners.

DAVE EGGERS

MY
FATHER
is my
shelter.

"

Fathering is not something
perfect men do, but something
that perfects the man.

FRANK PITTMAN

ONE FATHER IS MORE THAN A HUNDRED SCHOOLMASTERS.

GEORGE HERBERT

SOMETIMES THE POOREST MAN LEAVES HIS CHILDREN THE RICHEST INHERITANCE.

RUTH E. RENKEL

YOU KNOW YOU'RE A DAD WHEN...

... you're finally reading the pension and life insurance information your company sent you years ago

... you remain confident in your navigation skills, even when it's obvious you're completely lost

... you come back with snacks and a sports magazine when you were asked to do the weekly grocery shop

... you cry watching your child
in their school show

... you're not embarrassed to sing
(the wrong words) to a hip new
song on the radio

… you can't resist the urge to prove that you've "still got it" at any family event with a dance floor

… you always volunteer to help with homework – even though you have no idea what a square root is

I've made a few nice dishes in my time, but this has got to be the best one I've ever made.

JAMIE OLIVER ON HIS FIRST CHILD

ANY MAN CAN BE A FATHER, BUT IT TAKES SOMEONE SPECIAL TO BE A DAD.

ANONYMOUS

You're the

the

GLUE THAT
HOLDS US
ALL TOGETHER.

YOU DON'T RAISE HEROES, YOU RAISE SONS. AND IF YOU TREAT THEM LIKE SONS, THEY'LL TURN OUT TO BE HEROES, EVEN IF IT'S JUST IN YOUR OWN EYES.

WALTER SCHIRRA SR

Anyone who tells you fatherhood is the greatest thing that can happen to you, they are understating it.

MIKE MYERS

You inspire

ME TO BE
THE BEST
I CAN BE.

> I have found the best
> way to give advice to your
> children is to find out what
> they want and then advise
> them to do it.

HARRY S. TRUMAN

THE SOONER YOU TREAT YOUR SON AS A MAN, THE SOONER HE WILL BE ONE.

JOHN DRYDEN

MY MOTHER TAUGHT ME MY ABCs. FROM MY FATHER I LEARNED THE GLORIES OF GOING TO THE BATHROOM OUTSIDE.

LEWIS GRIZZARD

YOU ALWAYS

support

me.

YOUR DAD IS THE MAN WHO DOES ALL THE HEAVY SHOVELLING FOR YOUR SANDCASTLE AND THEN TELLS YOU YOU'VE DONE A WONDERFUL JOB.

ROSE O'KELLY

A father carries pictures where
his money used to be.

ANONYMOUS

THE WORDS THAT A FATHER SPEAKS TO HIS CHILDREN IN THE PRIVACY OF HOME ARE NOT HEARD BY THE WORLD, BUT... ARE CLEARLY HEARD AT THE END AND BY POSTERITY.

JEAN PAUL RICHTER

What we become depends on what our fathers teach us at odd moments, when they aren't trying to teach us.

UMBERTO ECO

I LOVE MY FATHER AS THE STARS — HE'S A BRIGHT SHINING EXAMPLE AND A HAPPY TWINKLING IN MY HEART.

TERRI GUILLEMETS

You urge me on

TO DO EVEN BETTER THAN MY BEST.

The mark of a good
parent is that he can have
fun while being one.

MARCELENE COX

YOU SHOW ME
HOW TO

embrace

life.

DAD ALWAYS CALLED ME HIS "FAVOURITE SON".

CAMERON DIAZ ON BEING A TOMBOY

By the time a man realizes that maybe his father was right, he usually has a son who thinks he's wrong.

CHARLES WADSWORTH

A FATHER IS A BANKER PROVIDED BY NATURE.

FRENCH PROVERB

NEVER PUT ANYTHING ON PAPER, MY BOY, AND NEVER TRUST A MAN WITH A SMALL BLACK MOUSTACHE.

P. G. WODEHOUSE QUOTING
HIS FATHER'S ADVICE TO HIM

YOU ARE THE
ONLY PERSON
who makes me
laugh until my
cheeks ache.

Child's definition of Father's Day:
"It's just like Mother's Day, only
you don't spend as much."

ANONYMOUS

It is a wise father that knows his own child.

WILLIAM SHAKESPEARE

I DON'T MIND LOOKING
INTO THE MIRROR AND
SEEING MY FATHER.

MICHAEL DOUGLAS

I wouldn't swap you for anything IN THE WORLD.

NO MAN I EVER MET WAS MY FATHER'S EQUAL, AND I NEVER LOVED ANY OTHER MAN AS MUCH.

HEDY LAMARR

The heart of a father is the masterpiece of nature.

ANTOINE-FRANÇOIS PRÉVOST D'EXILES

IF YOUR CHILDREN LOOK UP TO YOU, YOU'VE MADE A SUCCESS OF LIFE'S BIGGEST JOB.

ANONYMOUS

I cannot think of any need in childhood as strong as the need for a father's protection.

SIGMUND FREUD

Ways a dad will always embarrass his kid

He'll give them a kiss on the cheek in front of their friends when he drops them off at school

He sings at the top of his
voice and always gets
the words wrong

He'll tell jokes that only
he finds funny

He'll ask their new love interest embarrassing questions...

... or he'll bring up the time when they had to sleep with the light on after watching *Jurassic Park*

He'll wear something that stopped
fitting him 20 years ago –
in public, of course

He'll continue to refer to them by
their childhood nickname until
they're at least 40

Dad,
you're
someone

I LOOK UP TO
NO MATTER HOW
TALL I'VE GROWN.

YOUR CHILDREN
NEED YOUR
PRESENCE
MORE THAN
YOUR PRESENTS.

JESSE JACKSON

HE WAS A FATHER.
THAT'S WHAT A
FATHER DOES.
EASES THE
BURDENS OF
THOSE HE LOVES.

GEORGE SAUNDERS

"

I think my dad is a lot
cooler than other dads.
He still acts like he's still 17.

MILEY CYRUS

Great oaks from
little acorns grow.

ANONYMOUS

To the world,

YOU ARE A FATHER; TO YOUR FAMILY, YOU ARE THE WORLD.

THERE IS MORE TO
FATHERS THAN MEETS
THE EYE.

MARGARET ATWOOD

YOU CAN'T UNDERSTAND IT UNTIL YOU EXPERIENCE THE SIMPLE JOY OF THE FIRST TIME YOUR SON POINTS AT A SEAGULL AND SAYS "DUCK".

RUSSELL CROWE ON FATHERHOOD

The family is one of nature's masterpieces.

GEORGE SANTAYANA

ONLY A FATHER DOESN'T BEGRUDGE HIS SON'S TALENT.

JOHANN WOLFGANG VON GOETHE

You always lift

MY SPIRITS.

THE SECRET OF
FATHERHOOD
IS TO KNOW
WHEN TO STOP
TICKLING.

ANONYMOUS

Blessed indeed is the man
who hears many gentle
voices call him father.

LYDIA MARIA CHILD

THERE'S NO PILLOW QUITE SO SOFT AS A FATHER'S STRONG SHOULDER.

RICHARD L. EVANS

SECRET SKILLS THAT ONLY DADS KNOW

How to assemble anything, even
with Japanese instructions (who
reads instructions anyway?!)

How to lose convincingly
at every single game
he plays with his kid

How to fix his kid's stroller...
and their bike...
and their car

How to follow a movie's plotline,
despite having slept through
the whole thing

How to pull off the socks-sandals-
sunburn look in summer
(well, sort of...)

How to make his kids hear the call
for dinner, even if they're a
street away from home

How to break wind
and blame it on the
dog/cat/hamster/goldfish

A father's words are like a
thermostat that sets the
temperature in the house.

PAUL LEWIS

There are only two
lasting bequests we can
hope to give our children.
One of these is roots.
The other, wings.

HODDING CARTER

You're
IRREPLACEABLE.

FATHERLY LOVE IS THE ABILITY TO EXPECT THE BEST FROM YOUR CHILDREN DESPITE THE FACTS.

JASMINE BIRTLES

BEING A GREAT FATHER IS LIKE SHAVING. NO MATTER HOW GOOD YOU SHAVED TODAY, YOU HAVE TO DO IT AGAIN TOMORROW.

REED MARKHAM

Nothing could get at me if I
curled up on my father's lap...
All about him was safe.

NAOMI MITCHISON

WHAT DO I OWE MY FATHER? EVERYTHING.

HENRY VAN DYKE

To her, the name of father was another name for love.

FANNY FERN

CHARACTER IS LARGELY CAUGHT, AND THE FATHER AND THE HOME SHOULD BE THE GREAT SOURCES OF CHARACTER INFECTION.

FRANK H. CHELEY

AWARDS FOR
"THE BEST DAD EVER"

Bravery in the Face of Spiders and
Other Intimidating Creatures

Friendliest 24-hour Taxi Driver

Best Sean Connery (as James Bond) Impression

Champion Pancake Flipper

Giver of the Biggest Bear Hugs

Loudest Team Supporter

Maker of the Tastiest Sandwich

Lord of the (Dad) Dance

Bounciest Beer Belly

Best Bad Joke Teller

Master of DIY

Thank you
for the
example
you set me
EVERY DAY.

BEING A DAD IS MORE IMPORTANT THAN FOOTBALL, MORE IMPORTANT THAN ANYTHING.

DAVID BECKHAM

Nothing you do for
children is ever wasted.

GARRISON KEILLOR

My father used to say that it's never too late to do anything you wanted to do.

MICHAEL JORDAN

FAMILY IS NOT AN IMPORTANT THING. IT'S EVERYTHING.

MICHAEL J. FOX

Dad,

YOU'RE MY FAVOURITE PERSON.

He opened the jar of pickles
when no one else could.

ERMA BOMBECK ON HER DAD

THERE IS A SPECIAL PLACE IN HEAVEN FOR THE FATHER WHO TAKES HIS DAUGHTER SHOPPING.

JOHN SINOR

GETTING A BURP OUT OF YOUR LITTLE THING IS PROBABLY THE GREATEST SATISFACTION I'VE COME ACROSS.

BRAD PITT ON HIS FIRST CHILD

Silence is golden,

UNLESS YOU HAVE KIDS; THEN SILENCE IS SUSPICIOUS.

A father's solemn duty is to watch football with his children and teach them when to shout at the ref.

PAUL COLLINS

ARE WE NOT LIKE TWO VOLUMES OF ONE BOOK?

MARCELINE DESBORDES-VALMORE

Dads are most ordinary men turned by love into heroes, adventurers, storytellers, and singers of song.

PAM BROWN

I am lucky

TO HAVE A DAD WITH SUCH A GREAT SENSE OF HUMOUR.

NO MAN STANDS SO TALL AS WHEN HE STOOPS TO HELP A CHILD.

ANONYMOUS

THINGS FOUND IN DAD'S SHED

His secret shrine to his
favourite sports star

Twelve gallons of untouched
home-brew beer

A manual for a car he sold
15 years ago

The first chapter of a book-in-progress entitled *101 Uses for Used Batteries*

The novelty tie he got from Grandma as a birthday gift

His prized beer-bottle-top collection

A failed attempt at a DIY crystal radio

Well, it's hard to know
what to get the man who
provides everything.

MICHAEL FELDMAN ON RECEIVING A SET OF
HOSE NOZZLES ON FATHER'S DAY

A DAD IS SOMEONE WHO WANTS TO CATCH YOU BEFORE YOU FALL, BUT INSTEAD PICKS YOU UP, BRUSHES YOU OFF AND LETS YOU TRY AGAIN.

ANONYMOUS

I can do anything

BECAUSE I'VE

GOT YOU BY

MY SIDE.

WHILE WE TRY TO TEACH
OUR CHILDREN ALL
ABOUT LIFE, OUR
CHILDREN TEACH US
WHAT LIFE IS ALL ABOUT.

ANGELA SCHWINDT

Their absolute love of their children places them above the highest praise.

ANTON CHEKHOV ON HIS PARENTS

DADS GRAB THEMSELVES A SPOON AND DIG RIGHT IN WITH YOU.

ANONYMOUS

Ninety per cent

OF PARENTING
IS THINKING
ABOUT WHEN
YOU CAN LIE
DOWN AGAIN.

My father had a
profound influence
on me – he was
a lunatic.

SPIKE MILLIGAN

MY FATHER WAS AN AMAZING MAN. THE OLDER I GOT, THE SMARTER HE GOT.

ANONYMOUS

OUT OF ALL
THE REST,
MY DAD IS

the best.

FAMILY IS THE MOST IMPORTANT THING IN THE WORLD.

DIANA, PRINCESS OF WALES

When my father didn't have my hand... He had my back.

LINDA POINDEXTER

My father was my teacher.
But, most importantly,
he was a great dad.

BEAU BRIDGES

CHILDREN LEARN TO SMILE FROM THEIR PARENTS.

SHINICHI SUZUKI

YOU NEVER GET REALLY
GROSS WITH ME,
EVEN WHEN...

... I leave sticky fingerprints
· inside your car

... I flood the bathroom after leaving the water running

... my pet snail somehow finds its way into your shoe

... I use your favourite sweatshirt to wipe the dog down after a muddy walk

... I burn my toast (again!) and set off the smoke detector

... I seem incapable of adjusting
the volume of my speakers

... I call you up at 3 a.m.
to come and pick me up
from a party

A dad

IS A FRIEND
WHO WILL
NEVER LEAVE
YOU.

Infinite patience, boundless
enthusiasm, kindness,
the ability to score a goal...
and the strength to say "no"
every now and again.

DADS REGARD THEMSELVES AS GIANT SHOCK ABSORBERS, THERE TO PROTECT THE FAMILY FROM THE RUTS AND BUMPS ON THE ROAD OF LIFE.

W. BRUCE CAMERON

YOU WILL ALWAYS BE YOUR CHILD'S FAVOURITE TOY.

VICKI LANSKY

YOU HAVE YOUR SET
TIME FOR BEING A ROCK
'N' ROLL STAR... THEN
THERE'S GOING TO HAVE
TO BE TIMES SET ASIDE
FOR BEING DADDY AND
HAVING CHOCOLATE
RUBBED IN MY FACE.

NOEL GALLAGHER

My dad always had this little sign on his desk: "The bigger your head is, the easier your shoes are to fill."

PHIL JACKSON

NO LOVE IS GREATER THAN THAT OF A FATHER FOR HIS SON.

DAN BROWN

DAD, I DON'T KNOW WHAT I'D DO

without you.

My father's busy but he
always has time for me.

JUDY BLUME

Family: a social unit where the father is concerned with parking space, the children with outer space and the mother with closet space.

EVAN ESAR

IT IS AMAZING HOW QUICKLY THE KIDS LEARN TO DRIVE A CAR, YET ARE UNABLE TO UNDERSTAND THE LAWNMOWER, DISHWASHER OR VACUUM CLEANER.

BEN BERGOR

You
never
LET ME DOWN.

I LOVE MY DAD, ALTHOUGH I'M DEFINITELY CRITICAL OF HIM SOMETIMES, LIKE WHEN HIS PANTS ARE TOO TIGHT.

LIV TYLER

"

How sweet 'tis to sit 'neath
a fond father's smile.

JOHN HOWARD PAYNE

YOU'RE THE BEST
DAD BECAUSE...

... you take me on all the rides at
the theme park and don't complain
when you feel sick

... you never ask for that
money I "borrowed"

... you let me eat dinner in front
of the television

... you give the warmest hugs

... you always barbecue my
burger to perfection

... you let me do things
that Mum doesn't

... you let me make my
own mistakes

Papas should be loving their children so much that they cry when they gone.

ANDREW GALASETTI

YOU GIVE

the best

advice.

THANK YOU
FOR BEING...

Dad in a million!

If you're interested in finding out more about our books, find us on Facebook at Summersdale Publishers and follow us on Twitter at @Summersdale.

www.summersdale.com